Enchanted

Forest

Activity
Book

ARCTURUS

ARCTURUS

This edition published in 2023 by Arcturus Publishing Limited
26/27 Bickels Yard, 151–153 Bermondsey Street,
London SE1 3HA

Illustrator: Sam Loman
Author: Lisa Regan
Editor: Violet Peto
Design: Well Nice Ltd
Managing Editor: Joe Harris

ISBN: 978-1-3988-2558-1
CH008279NT
Supplier 29, Date 1122, PI 00001954

Printed in China

PIXIE PARTY

Help the pixie get to the party by following
the arrows in the correct direction each time.

Start

Finish

Beautiful Birds

How many birds have a yellow beak, a blue tail, and pink on their wings?

Do You Doodle?

Let your imagination run wild with a wonderful unicorn doodle in this enchanted forest scene. Use your brightest pens, crayons, or pencils.

A BUSY DAY

Susie Squirrel has promised to visit her friend in the morning, collect acorns at lunchtime, say hello to Owl in the afternoon, and be back home to her babies by dinner. In what order should she follow the paths?

	Green hat	Red hat	Blue hat
Freddy			
George			
Luca			

Heigh-Ho

It's off to work they go ... use the clues to figure out which job is done by each gnome and what each one is wearing.

	Gardener	Builds roads	Builds houses
Freddy			
George			
Luca			

The gnome with a blue hat builds houses.

Freddy builds roads for a living.

Luca plants flowers for his job. His hat isn't green.

George doesn't have a red hat.

7

Fairy Finds

Do you know where fairies live?
Use the grid code to discover the answer.

B2.D4.D4 / B2.C1.B3.A1.D3.D2 / C4.B3.A1

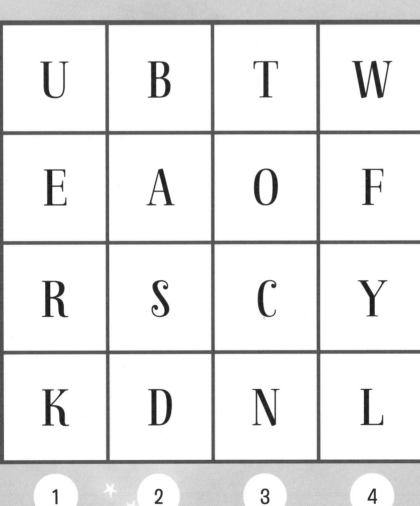

	1	2	3	4
A	U	B	T	W
B	E	A	O	F
C	R	S	C	Y
D	K	D	N	L

_ _ _   _ _ _ _ _ _   _ _ _

Let It Glow

Which of the magical fireflies
is one of a kind?

It's a Mix-Up

Rearrange the letters on each leaf. Which one doesn't spell the word MAGICAL?

1 AGMICAL

2 AGICMAL

3 GICELAM

4 CALGAMI

5 MLAICGA

6 GACLAIM

Winter Wonderland

The forest looks even more enchanting when snow has fallen.
Can you spot eight differences between these snowy scenes?

Mysterious Message

The elves often communicate to each other with messages in the mud. Can you figure out what this one says?

_____ _____ _____

_____ _____ _____ _____

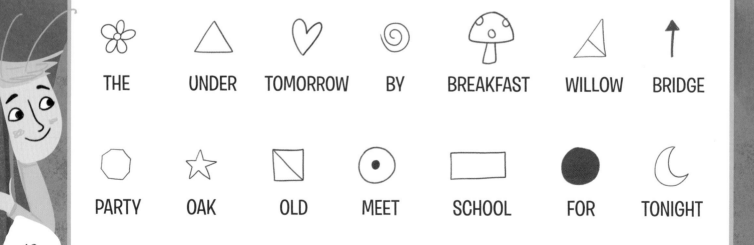

❀	△	♡	◎	🍄	◁	↑
THE	UNDER	TOMORROW	BY	BREAKFAST	WILLOW	BRIDGE
⬡	☆	◻	◉	▭	⬤	☾
PARTY	OAK	OLD	MEET	SCHOOL	FOR	TONIGHT

In a Twist

How many new words containing three or more letters can you make out of the enchanted forest phrase?

TANGLED TREES

IN THE SHADOWS

Which of the silhouettes is an exact match for this wood sprite, who is flitting between the trees?

Leafy Labyrinth

Find a way through the tangled maze to reach
the enchanted door in the middle.

Start

Finish

Forest Hideaway

It's amazing what you can stumble across in an enchanted forest! Look carefully to find each of the items from the panel in the big picture.

Who Am I?

Cross out all the letters that appear twice. Use the letters that are left to spell a type of creature that lives in the enchanted forest.

M S P M R I A T O

O A E D F N D F N

Let's Draw!

Learn to draw a darling deer
by following the steps.

1

2

3

4

Fun in the Sun

The elves are having a wonderful time playing together.
Can you use these clues to find some of them?

Ellena has a daisy chain in her hair.

Luna is climbing onto the swing.

Freya is on the swing.

Eric is standing on the toadstool.

Forest Finds

Look in the string of letters for five forest creatures.
Use the leftover letters to spell this fairy's name.

RABBIT M F O X I S Q U I R R E L M D E E R S O W L Y

_____

Elfie Selfie

The elves just love taking selfies! Which of these pictures is slightly different from the others?

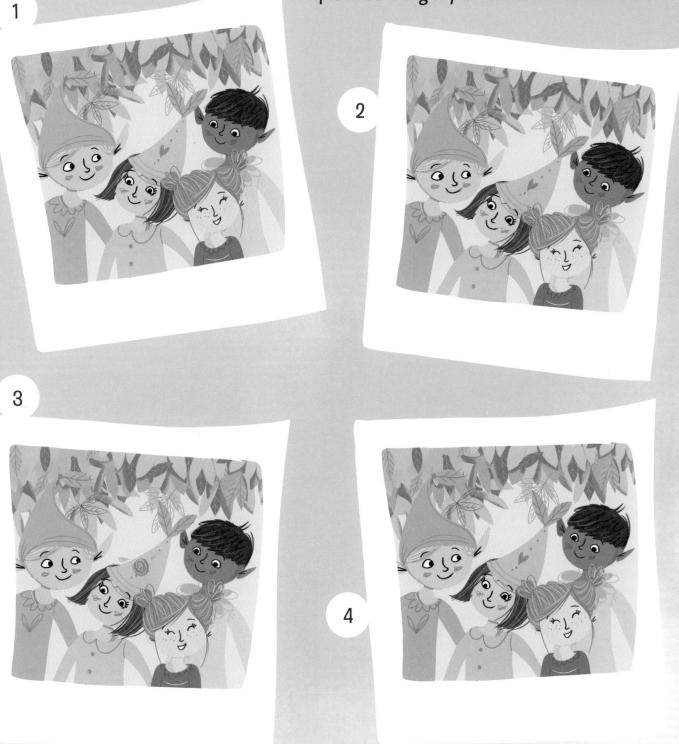

Jumbled Up

There is an unusual house in the enchanted forest with lots and lots of people living there! Each has left their shoes lying around. Can you pair them up and find an odd shoe somewhere?

Home Sweet Home

It's amazing what is hidden in the heart of the enchanted forest! Finish the picture with your pens and crayons.

Hidden Gems

The forest is home to this little dragon and her collection of gems. Can you find this pattern in her treasure trove?

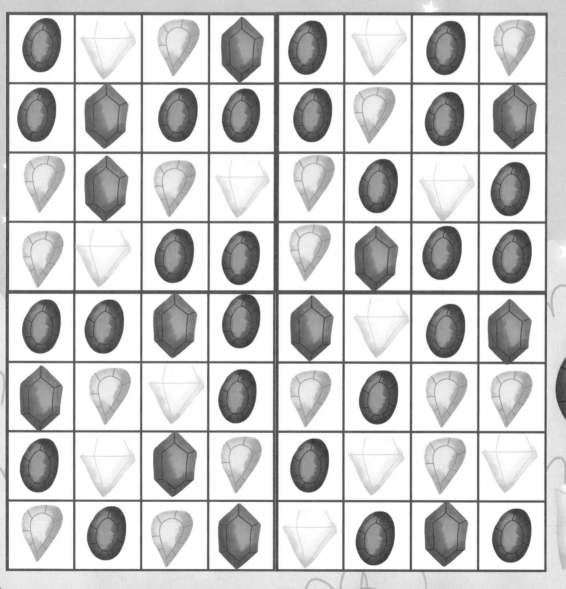

Snail Trail

Which snail has taken the longest route—A, B, or C?
Follow their paths to find out.

Feathered Friends

Each of these birds has a matching twin, except one.
Which bird is on its own?

Doodle-Do!

Add more flowers and fairies to this enchanted scene.

Shining Lights

Darkness has fallen in the forest. That means it's time for the fairy folk to light up the night! Can you spot eight differences between these two pictures?

Let's Draw!

Learn to draw a happy gnome
by following the steps.

1

2

3

4

31

Raindrop Runaround

Which impish elf is the odd one out?

Fluttery Night

Can you guide the firefly to its mate? Follow the arrows in the correct direction each time, and don't get distracted by the other fireflies and their flashing!

Start

Finish

We Heart Stars

The enchanted forest is the perfect
home for this herd of unicorns.
How many white stars are there?

Shadowy Statue

Which of the silhouettes is an
exact match for this statue in
the heart of the forest?

A

B

C

D

Funny Bunnies

Which of these bunnies is named Sonny? He has one white ear, one brown ear, and a pink nose.

Words of Wisdom

The fairies want to share their secrets!
Use the grid code to discover what their advice is.

B4.C2.A1.C3.D1 / D1.A3.D1.D4.B1 / B4.C2.B1

	1	2	3	4
A	N	S	V	P
B	Y	O	L	D
C	K	A	C	G
D	E	T	F	R

_ _ _ _ _   _ _ _ _ _   _ _ _

Rainbow Maze

Fiona the flying pony is looking for the gold at the end of the rainbow. Guide her through the maze to find the treasure!

Start

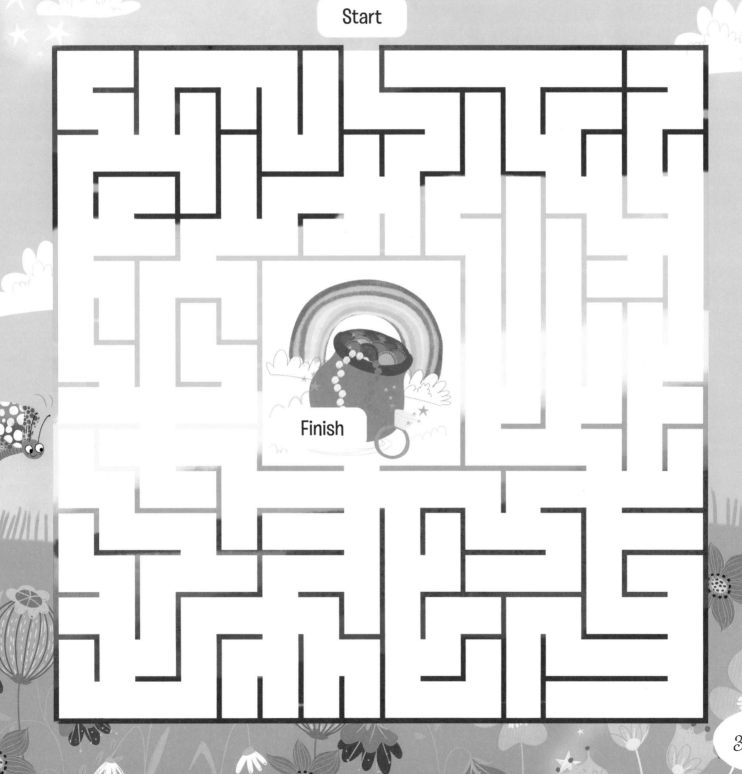

Finish

Who Goes There?

Cross out all the letters that appear twice.
Use the letters that are left to spell a type of
creature that hides in the trees.

A N A G Y M G B

B P H S O S O

Winter Wonderland

It is snowing in the forest, and the pixies are having fun! Which snowflake doesn't match any of the others?

Pixie Papers

Pebble the Pixie has written a note for his friend.
Can you find out what the message says?

FOR | TELL | SQUIRREL | KEEP | TONIGHT | PRESENT | TOMORROW

IT | EVERYONE | RABBIT | SECRET | MIDNIGHT | OWL | PARTY

Watch Out!

How many new words containing three or more letters can you make out of the enchanted forest phrase?

BEWARE OF THE TROLL

Motherly Love

Which of the rabbit's babies is a tiny bit different from the others?

The More the Merrier

These unicorns are getting ready for a special day with their friends. Decorate them so that they look their best.

Finding Food

Help Susie Squirrel find all 15 acorns in this forest scene, and then finish the picture with your pens and crayons.

1

Let's Draw!

Learn to draw an enchanted castle by following the steps.

2

4

3

47

Watery World

This enchanted forest is home to a family of water sprites.
Look carefully to find each of the items in the big picture.

1 AENNTECHD

2 ANENCDHTE

3 EDNTECHAN

All Mixed Up

Rearrange the letters on each star. Which one of them doesn't spell the word ENCHANTED?

5 EANTEDNCO

4 CHENDANTE

6 HENDECANT

Moondrop

Florabell

Fairy Glade

Which are there more of, moondrops or florabells?

Flossie's home has a pink door and round windows.

Maria's home has round windows and flowers outside.

Fleur lives in a toadstool with eight white spots on the roof.

Nico has decorated his home with stripes.

Daisy's house has square windows and a crooked chimney.

Belle has planted yellow flowers outside her home.

FAIRY FOREST

This part of the forest is home to the fairies. Find out who lives where using the clues.

Antoine lives behind a green door with ivy around it.

Pierre's house has three windows and yellow curtains.

Daisy Chain

Which fairy scene is the odd one out?

54

Dream Dwelling

Look at this house nestled in the heart of the forest!
Make it look even more tasty by finishing it with your
pens and crayons.

What a Hoot!

Which two of these owls match each other exactly?

Let's Draw!

Learn to draw a toadstool house by following the steps.

1

2

3

4

57

Magical Map

Use the grid on the map to answer the questions and find your way around the enchanted forest.

1. Who lives in the house in square D3?

2. Which square has the shoe house?

3. Where are the pine trees?

4. Which of these squares has no house in it: C4, B3, or D2?

5. Where is the best place for picking flowers?

6. Who lives in C2 and C3?

RING O' ROSES

Have you ever seen a fairy ring? This one is perfect for dancing around!

Can you spot eight differences between these two pictures?

Perfect Princess

This enchanted princess lives in the forest. Finish the picture with your pens and crayons.

A Gem of a Find

The enchanted forest is home to many magical creatures, including this emerald dragon. Which of the silhouettes is an exact match for the picture of the beautiful beast?

A

B

C

D

Run Away!

Escape from the tree troll by following the arrows
in the correct directions each time. Quick!

Finish

Start

Hide-and-Seek

Look in the string of letters
for six enchanted creatures.
Use the leftover letters to
spell a type of tree.

GNOMEWPIXIEIELFLFAIRYLDRAGONOSPRITEW

Falling Leaves

Which of the leaves is one of a kind?

Forest Friends

Which of the wood sprites is a tiny bit
different from the others?

In a Grump!

Let's throw a party to cheer up these wood sprites.
Use your pens and crayons to add happy creatures
and decorations.

Fairy Advice

What are the fairies trying to tell you? Use the grid code to discover the answer.

A1.B3.D4 / A3.B1.C2.D1 / A2.D1.B3.C4.A4.C1
B2.B4.A3 / D2.C3.D3.D2

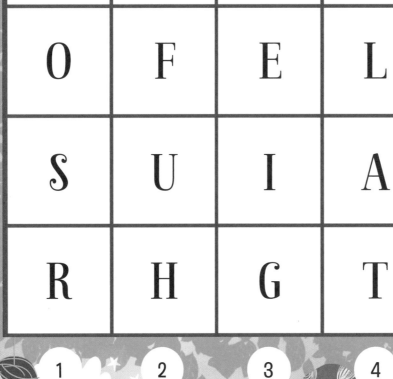

	1	2	3	4
A	L	D	Y	M
B	O	F	E	L
C	S	U	I	A
D	R	H	G	T

_ _ _   _ _ _ _   _ _ _ _ _ _

_ _ _   _ _ _ _

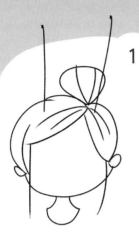

Let's Draw!

Learn to draw a fairy by following the steps.

1

2

3

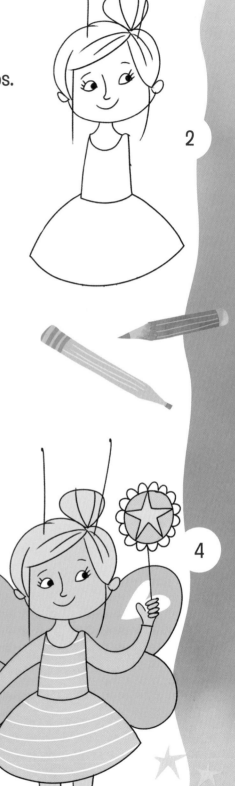

4

69

Flower Power

Muriel needs to collect a special type of flower for her magic spell. How many can you find that look exactly like this one?

Flower Fairies

Help the fairy out of the flower maze without disturbing
any of the busy bees on the way.

Start

Finish

Through the Keyhole

Cross out all the letters that appear twice. Use the letters that
are left to spell out who lives in this little house.

YHSHYSGAN
OAMRERTT

A Snowy Scene

How many new words containing three or more letters can you make out of this enchanted forest phrase?

WINTER WONDERLAND

Sprite Secrets

The water sprites are speaking in code. Use the translation device to figure out what they are saying.

_____ _____ _____ _____ _____

HIDE	PRESENT	THE	FOOD	RABBIT	MAKING	FROM

LET	TELL	IS	MISCHIEF	OUTSIDE	BEGIN	NAUGHTY

How Does Your Garden Grow?

What a beautiful enchanted garden! Finish the picture using your pens and crayons.

Going to the Ball

This fairy is getting ready to party! Can you spot eight differences between these two pictures? Finish the pictures yourself with pens or crayons.

Home from Home

Which of these would be your enchanted home?
Use your name to find out.

1. Write down your full name, and count how many letters are in it.

2. Are there more than nine letters? If so, add the digits together to make a single number.

3. Use your answer to see which of the homes is yours!

1

2

3

4

5

6

7

8

9

Runaway Rabbits

Use the clues to help you put a name next to each of the rabbits.

Theo has an eye patch which is not brown.
Cookie has a black tail and black ears.
Binky is brown with a pink nose.
Louie has one brown ear and one white ear.
Turbo is white with a black tail.
Sage is completely white.
Milo is black with white ears.
Sniffles has brown ears and a brown tail.

Let's Draw!

Learn to draw a magical unicorn
by following the steps.

1

2

3

4

79

On Top of the World

One magical tree in the forest leads to a wonderful world above! Look carefully to find each of the items in the big picture.

Beautiful Creatures

Rearrange each bird's letters.
Which one of them doesn't spell
the word GORGEOUS?

ORGEOGUS

A

B

ORGEGEOS

C

SURGEGOO

D

GOOGERUS

REGOSUGO

OOGREGUS

E

F

Shine a Light

Study the sequence of each lantern string, and find out
which one or two should go next in the white boxes

83

Cover to Cover

Which little fairy picture is the odd one out?

A Dreamy Doodle

What is the wood sprite dreaming about? You decide!

Forest Family

Which of the silhouettes is an exact match for this deer and her precious fawn?

A

B

C

D

Words of Wisdom

Shade in all the boxes that contain the letters M, U, and D. The remaining letters spell out a piece of advice for strangers to the forest.

M	M	U	D	D	U	D	M	U	U
D	S	M	M	T	M	A	D	D	Y
D	U	D	U	U	M	D	M	U	D
M	D	O	D	D	N	M	U	D	U
U	M	U	D	M	U	M	D	U	D
M	T	D	H	M	D	E	M	U	D
M	U	D	D	D	U	D	M	D	U
M	U	M	U	P	D	A	D	M	M
D	D	U	D	U	D	D	T	H	U
M	U	D	M	U	M	M	U	D	D

87

Bird-oku

Finish the bird-themed sudoku grid by filling in the missing pictures. Each picture should appear only once in each row, column, and mini-grid.

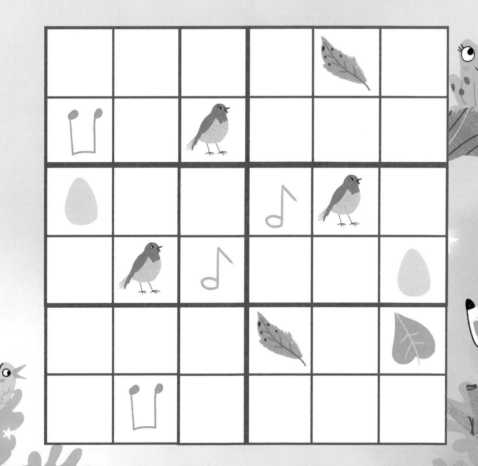

Answers

Page 3

Page 4

Page 6

Susie Squirrel should follow the paths in this order:

B – Visit her friend in the morning.
D – Collect acorns at lunchtime.
A – Say hello to Owl in the afternoon.
C – Be back home to her babies by supper.

Page 7

	Green hat	Red hat	Blue hat
Freddy	✓		
George			✓
Luca		✓	

	Gardener	Builds roads	Builds houses
Freddy		✓	
George			✓
Luca	✓		

The gnome with a blue hat builds houses.

Freddy builds roads for a living.

Luca plants flowers for his job. His hat isn't green.

George doesn't have a red hat.

Page 8

B2.D4.D4 / B2.C1.B3.A1.D3.D2 / C4.B3.A1

	1	2	3	4
A	U	B	T	W
B	E	A	O	F
C	R	S	C	Y
D	K	D	N	L

A L L   A R O U N D   Y O U

Page 9

Page 10

1 AGMICAL
2 AGICMAL
3 GICELAM
4 CALGAMI
5 MLAICGA
6 GACLAIM

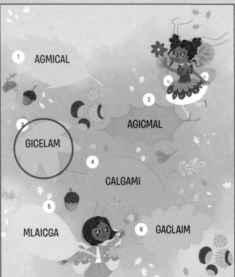

Page 11

Page 12

Page 13

TANGLED TREES
Here are some words you
might have thought of:

set	let	street
rest	net	age
nest	sent	desert
get	ten	
leg		

Page 14

Page 15

Pages 16–17

Page 18

Pages 20–21

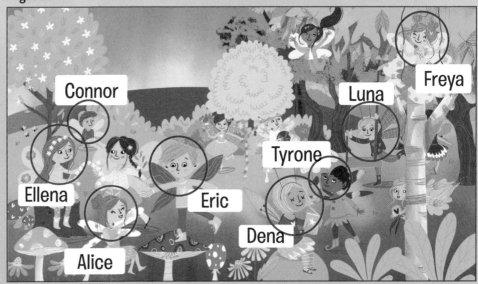

90

Page 22

MIMSY

Page 23

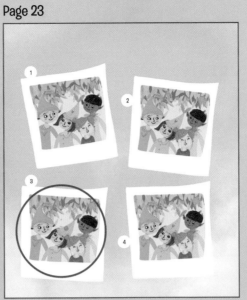

Page 24

Page 26

Page 27

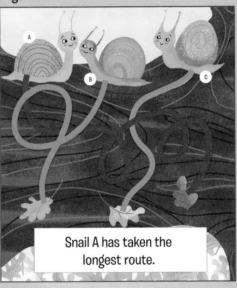

Snail A has taken the longest route.

Page 28

Page 30

Page 32

Page 33

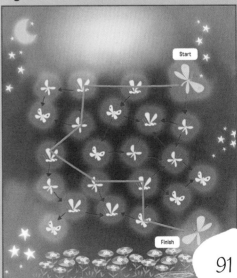

Start

Finish

91

Pages 34–35 There are 21 white stars.

Page 36

Page 37

Page 38

B4.C2.A1.C3.D1 / D1.A3.D1.D4.B1 / B4.C2.B1

	1	2	3	4
A	N	S	V	P
B	Y	O	L	D
C	K	A	C	G
D	E	T	F	R

DANCE EVERY DAY

Page 39

Start

Finish

Page 40

ANAGYMGB
BPHSOSO
NYMPH

Page 41

Page 42

PARTY TOMORROW FOR OWL

KEEP IT SECRET

FOR	TELL	SQUIRREL	KEEP	TONIGHT	PRESENT	TOMORROW
IT	EVERYONE	RABBIT	SECRET	MIDNIGHT	OWL	PARTY

Page 43

BEWARE OF THE TROLL

Here are some words you might have thought of:

few
feel
her
loft
row
wolf
roll
throw
fell
hotel
lower
floor

Page 44

Page 46 There are 15 acorns.

Pages 48–49

Page 50

AENNTECHD
ANENCDHTE
EDNTECHAN
CHENDANTE
EANTEDNCO
HENDECANT

Page 51 There are more florabells.

6
8

Pages 52–53

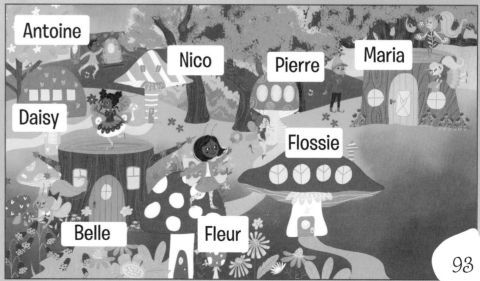

Antoine
Nico
Pierre
Maria
Daisy
Flossie
Belle
Fleur

Page 54

Page 56

Pages 58–59

1. Who lives in the house in square D3? **Squirrels**
2. Which square has the shoe house? **B4**
3. Where are the pine trees? **B2**
4. Which of these squares has no house in it? **B3**
5. Where is the best place for picking flowers? **A2**
6. Who lives in C2 and C3? **Water sprites**

Page 60

Page 62

Page 63

Finish

Start

Page 64

WILLOW

94

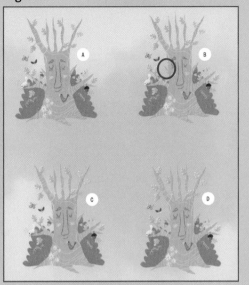

A1.B3.D4 / A3.B1.C2.D1 / A2.D1.B3.C4.A4.C1 / B2.B4.A3 / D2.C3.D3.D2

	1	2	3	4
A	L	D	Y	M
B	O	F	E	L
C	S	U	I	A
D	R	H	G	T

LET YOUR DREAMS FLY HIGH

There are 10 magical flowers.

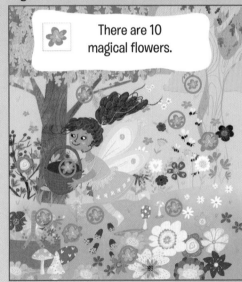

Finish

Start

YHSHYSGAN OAMRERTT

GNOME

WINTER WONDERLAND

Here are some words you might have thought of:

ten
wild   worn
      den   win
   went
end   world   drew
   twin   new   window

LET   THE   MISCHIEF   MAKING   BEGIN

HIDE   PRESENT   THE   FOOD   RABBIT   MAKING   FROM

LET   TELL   IS   MISCHIEF   OUTSIDE   BEGIN   NAUGHTY

95

Page 78

Pages 80–81

Page 82

ORGEOGUS
A
ORGEGEOS
B
SURGEGOO
C
GOOGERUS
D
OOGREGUS
E
REGOSUGO
F

Page 83

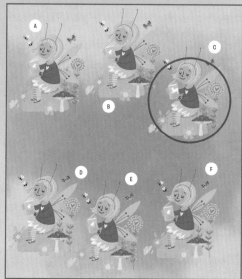

Page 84

Page 86

Page 87

STAY ON THE PATH

M	M	U	D	D	D	U	D	M	U	U
D	S	M	M	T	M	A	D	D	Y
D	U	D	U	U	M	D	M	U	D
M	D	O	D	D	N	M	U	D	U
U	M	U	D	M	U	M	D	U	D
M	T	D	H	M	E	M	U	D
M	U	D	D	D	U	D	M	D	U
M	U	M	U	P	D	A	D	M	M
D	D	U	D	U	D	T	H	U
M	U	D	M	U	M	M	U	D	D

Page 88

96